FOR THE LOVE OF
GOD

God's Unconditional Love

LEVONDA G. BROWN

DEDICATION

I dedicate this book…

To my Lord and Savior, Jesus Christ, who is the head of my life. I thank You for choosing to love me even when I did not know, deserve, or understand the true value and commitment of *unconditional* **love**.

To my loving husband, Kenneth, who is my best friend and confidant. I thank God for giving me a godly man who is a wonderful and devoted father. I love you unconditionally and pray you continue to grow in God.

To my loving children: Timothy and Krystal. I am so blessed and thankful that God chose me to be your mom. It is my prayer that you and your families continue to grow strong in the Lord and allow Him always to direct your paths. I love you all unconditionally.

To my parents, who decided to train me in the Word of God. I thank you for the discipline and correction directed towards me. I appreciate and love you dearly and unconditionally.

TABLE OF CONTENTS

INTRODUCTION

So many times, I hear people say that God always prepares you for the storm or challenge before it comes. I found this to be true several years ago. I felt the Holy Spirit urging me to begin a study on love.

I was studying relationships and the importance of having God in the center, but somehow it was not enough. Initially, I ignored the prompting and continued my studies. However, I could not shake it off, and the topic would not dissipate. Finally, I yielded to the yearnings and began studying the topic of love. I ordered a devotion on love by Kenneth and Gloria Copeland as well as several books and audio material on love relationships by several anointed authors in the Word ministry. The information and revelation gleaned from the various anointed authors provided great insight into how much God truly loves and cares about me. It was not what I could do for Him (God) but how much He cared for me to give His Son (Jesus) so that I could experience Eden as He intended each of us to have from day one of creation.

It is my prayer that you will appreciate God's love and move to act on it so others may know that the doing or behavior does not determine how much God loves us. It is the decision God made before the foundation of the world to love us unconditionally. He wants to show His love, shower us with blessings, and help us walk in "The Blessing". The requirement for us is to believe, receive, and act.

CHAPTER 1

How Do I Know That God Loves Me?

The one thing I came to realize is that my fulfillment is not in anyone or anything here on this earth. I love my husband, children, grandchildren, family, and friends, and there are things I enjoy. However, if all that would go away, I would not feel empty because I have God in my life, and I know He loves me (1 John 4:19). Colossians 2:10 tells me that I am complete in Him (God). Essentially, in God, I have everything I need. This may sound crazy or immature. Nonetheless, I fully believe that with God, I can conquer any obstacle or situation that I encounter. 1 John 5:4–5 (CEV) says,

> Every child of God can defeat the world,
> and our faith is what gives us this victory.
> No one can defeat the world without hav-
> ing faith in Jesus as the Son of God.

The Message translation says,

> Every God-born person conquers the world's ways. The conquering power that brings the world to its knees is our faith.

The person who wins out over the world's
ways is simply the one who believes Jesus
is the Son of God.

The conquering spirit I have is knowing that God loves
me, and when I put my trust in Him, His faith, and His
accomplishments, I am victorious. God loved the world
(me) so much that He decided to give His only Son to re-
deem the world (me) back to Him (John 3:16). He wants
me to have a life filled with abundance and joy to the full—
— *"I came that they may have and enjoy life, and have it
in abundance (to the full, till it overflows)"* (John 10:10b
AMPC). God desires for my abundance to overflow so that
I am instrumental in helping someone else realize their
abundant living in God or the abundant living they could
have in Him.

I am reminded of a passage from Kenneth and Gloria
Copeland's *Limitless Love* devotion that talks about one's
worth.[1] My worth is wrapped in the decision Jesus made to
give His life for me. Since Jesus became the propitiation
or ransom for my sins, it lets me know that He truly loves
me. I had nothing to give, and yet Jesus decided to give
His life for me. His sacrifice of becoming sin for me settled
once and for all my self-worth. This is how I know that

---

1 Kenneth Copeland and Gloria Copeland, *Limitless Love: A 365-Day Devotional,*
Updated edition (Harrison House Publishers, 2012, 258).

God loves me. My sinful nature made me feel worthless, invaluable, and condemned. My future was not bright. However, accepting Jesus as my Lord and Savior enabled me to see my worth and value through the eyes of God, the Father. There is no need to reference my performance, possessions, or any position I may endure to determine my worth. All I must do is remember the finished works Jesus completed (death, burial, resurrection, ascension, and now seated on the right hand of the Father) and know that my worth to God is as much as Jesus' worth because God gave Jesus in exchange for me. In other words, God forever established my worth in the blood of Jesus, His firstborn.

Because Jesus decided to give His life for me, once I believed, confessed, and accepted Him as my Lord and Savior, I am a joint heir with Jesus Christ (Romans 8:17). My newness of life is in Him. I am to rest in His finished works by maintaining all that He obtained for me.

In another passage from the same devotion book, *Limitless Love*, Brother Copeland shares how God demonstrated His love of commitment towards Abraham by making a blood covenant.[2]

When Abram was ninety-nine years old, the LORD appeared to him and said, "I am

---

2 Ibid, 206.

El-Shaddai—'God Almighty.' Serve me
faithfully and live a blameless life. I will
make a covenant with you, by which I will
guarantee to give you countless descen-
dants." At this, Abram fell face down on
the ground. Then God said to him, "This is
my covenant with you: I will make you the
father of a multitude of nations!

(Genesis 17:1–4 NLT)

In these verses, God, through this blood covenant, tells Abraham that He will care for and *bless* him. God did not make this commitment conditional. He did not say to Abraham *if you love me or do well towards me, I will **bless** you.* No, God simply lets Abraham know that His treatment or determination to *bless* him is not based on how he (Abraham) responds. God decided to love Abraham, regardless of Abraham's actions towards Him. In Romans 4:16–21 (KJV):

Therefore it is of faith, that it might be by
grace; to the end the promise might be
sure to all the seed; not to that only which
is of the law, but to that also which is of
the faith of Abraham; who is the father of
us all, (As it is written, I have made thee a
father of many nations,) before him whom

he believed, even God, who quickeneth the
dead, and calleth those things which be
not as though they were. Who against hope
believed in hope, that he might become the
father of many nations; according to that
which was spoken, So shall thy seed be.
And being not weak in faith, he considered
not his own body now dead, when he was
about an hundred years old, neither yet the
deadness of Sarah's womb: He staggered
not at the promise of God through unbelief; but was strong in faith, giving glory
to God; And being fully persuaded that,
what he had promised, he was able also to
perform.

Abraham fully trusted God to do what He said because
of the blood covenant God established between the two
of them and changing his name from Abram to Abraham
(see Genesis 17:4–7). This example lets me, as a believer,
know that to be like God and walk or operate the way He
does, God desires me to honor the blood covenant of Jesus
in the same manner unconditionally. I am held accountable
for my words and deeds, irrespective of how any person
responds or treats me. Therefore, my worth must remain
in God, and knowing that I am valued by Him, I can love
with the Godkind of love unconditionally.

CHAPTER 2

What Is the Difference? (Unconditional Love vs. Conditional Love)

As believers, we know that we are in the world, but indeed, we are not to act like the world (John 15:19, 17:14–16). Essentially, we are not to do as the world does when it comes to exemplifying love. As disciples of Christ, we must do and walk in love designed by God. Jesus lets us know that He was hated and, therefore, we will be hated in the world (John 15:18–19). Since we are ambassadors for Christ (2 Corinthians 5:20), we must represent Him in the manner presented in the Word of God. Matthew 5:14–16 reminds us that we are the light of the world. We are seen as a city that sits on a hill and is not hidden. We must decide to draw people to Christ by shining our light and not cause them to move further away.

Jesus illustrates the importance of shining our light in Luke 6:27–36. He starts by telling us to love our enemies and do good to them. Who are our enemies? If you have not believed in your heart and confessed with your mouth that Jesus is your Lord and Savior and asked Him to come into your heart and forgive you of your sins, you are an enmity to God and, therefore, an enemy to believers (Ephesians 2:12–19; James 4:4–7).

In simple terms, our enemies are anyone who has not accepted Jesus Christ as Lord and Savior and, therefore, cannot walk in the agape love or God's love. These individuals without Christ are allowing the enemy to operate or flow through them. They may be good people and do good things, but they are still an enmity to God because they have not accepted His Son, Jesus, into their hearts to be Lord and Savior over them. We (believers) must be bold enough not to retaliate against these individuals or groups but take a stand against the force behind their actions. If we decide or only show kindness, mercy, or love toward people we love or are in good standing with us, we are no different from the world (Luke 6:32–34). We are not shining our lights or exhibiting a difference.

The *American Dictionary of the English Language* describes the difference between conditional and unconditional. *Conditional* is defined as…

> Containing or depending on a condition or conditions; made with limitations; not absolute; made or granted on certain terms.
> A conditional promise is one which is to be

16

performed when something else stipulated is done or has taken place.[3]

Conversely, *unconditional* is defined as...

Absolute; unreserved; not limited by any conditions. We are required to make an unconditional surrender of ourselves to our Maker. The king demanded unconditional submission.[4]

Based on this unconditional definition and what has been shared thus far about God, who is love, *unconditional love* is simply unrestricted; affection or love without any limitations; not based on behavior; a decision to love or show affection regardless of what the recipient says or does.[5]

In its purest sense, love is a decision or choice. It is not a feeling. 1 John 4:7–10 (NLT) says,

Dear friends, let us continue to love one another, for love comes from God. Anyone who loves is a child of God and knows God. But anyone who does not love does

---

3 Noah Webster, "Conditional," in *Noah Webster American Dictionary of the English Language: Websters Online Dictionary 1828*, 2022, https://webstersdictionary1828. com/Dictionary/Conditional.
4 Noah Webster, "Unconditional," in *Noah Webster American Dictionary of the English Language: Websters Online Dictionary 1828*, 2022, https://webstersdictionary1828. com/Dictionary/unconditional.
5 Ibid.

not know God, for God is love. God
showed how much he loved us by sending
his one and only Son into the world so that
we might have eternal life through him.
This is real love—not that we loved God,
but that he loved us and sent his Son as a
sacrifice to take away our sins.

Love defined here talks about the character of God. Therefore, once we accept Jesus into our hearts and confess with our mouths salvation (total deliverance, completeness), we now have the Godkind of love residing in us, known as agape or unconditional love. There is no performance or behavioral act we need to do to get God to love us. His love was decided for us before the foundation of the world (see Ephesians 1:4). Since God is love, He created the world to display His love.

In the beginning, God created everything man would need before He created man and placed him in the Garden of Eden. Everything man needed was in the Garden. God displayed to man His unrestricted and unqualified love. There was nothing that man did or could do to earn this love. God gave it freely because He wanted mankind to know that He is willing and able to take care of every need, desire, and want.

The unconditional love presented by God is not a con. This unconditional love is what God did for the world. He decided to love us, and because of His unconditional, unrestricted love towards us, He gave His one and only Son to die for our sins to reconcile us back to Him. He had Jesus to take our place. God needed a sinless ram to become sin for us all. *"For he hath made him to be sin for us, who knew no sin; that we might be made the righteousness of God in him"* (2 Corinthians 5:21 KJV). Jesus was willing to become that sinless ram for us.

Wherefore when he cometh into the world, he saith, Sacrifice and offering thou wouldest not, but a body hast thou prepared me: In burnt offerings and sacrifices for sin thou hast had no pleasure. Then said I, Lo, I come (in the volume of the book it is written of me,) to do thy will, O God. Above when he said, Sacrifice and offering and burnt offerings and offering for sin thou wouldest not, neither hadst pleasure therein; which are offered by the law; Then said he, Lo, I come to do thy will, O God. He taketh away the first, that he may establish the second. By the which will we are sanctified through the offering of the body of Jesus Christ once for all. And every priest standeth daily ministering and offering oftentimes the same sacrifices, which can never take away sins: But this man, after he had offered one sacrifice for sins for ever, sat down on the right hand of God; From henceforth expecting till his enemies be made his footstool. For by one offering he hath perfected for ever them that are sanctified. Whereof the Holy Ghost also is a witness to us: for after that he had said before, This is the covenant that I will make with them after those days, saith the Lord, I will put my laws into their hearts, and in their minds will I write them; And their sins and iniquities will I remember no more. Now where remission of these is, there is no more offering for sin. Having therefore, brethren, boldness to enter into the holiest by the blood of Jesus, By a new and living way, which he hath consecrated for us, through the veil, that is to say, his flesh; And having an high priest over the house of God; Let us draw near with a true heart in full assurance of faith, having our hearts sprinkled from an evil conscience, and our bodies washed with pure water.

(Hebrews 10:5–22 KJV)

Conversely, conditional love is a con or ploy. This type of love is restricted, and one must qualify to earn or become a recipient of this love. Conditional love hinges on doing something to get something in return. The worldly term is *"quid pro quo"*. Essentially, you do for someone in exchange for something. If the agreement is not satisfied or fulfilled, then the exchange does not happen. Conditional love is based on performance.

How did we get here? *By living outside of perfect or unconditional love.*

> And God said, Let us make man in our image, after our likeness: and let them have dominion over the fish of the sea, and over the fowl of the air, and over the cattle, and over all the earth, and over every creeping thing that creepeth upon the earth. So God created man in his own image, in the image of God created he him; male and female created he them. And God blessed them, and God said unto them, Be fruitful, and multiply, and replenish the earth, and subdue it: and have dominion over the fish of the sea, and over the fowl of the air, and over every living thing that moveth upon the earth.

(Genesis 1:26–28 KJV)

In the beginning, God created a beautiful place for Adam (man) to live. God had a blank canvas and prepared everything for Adam before placing him in the Garden of Eden. God created man in His image and after His likeness and gave Man dominion over all the earth (Genesis 1:26). God's instructions to mankind were to be fruitful, multiply, replenish the earth, and subdue it (Genesis 1:28). Unfortunately, one day in the Garden of Eden, Adam committed high treason. The woman (Eve) was deceived (Genesis 3:13). The only law was for them not to eat of the tree of good and evil that was amid the garden. *One might say this was the tithe*—tithe for being under God's care. Regardless, Adam disobeyed, and the result was sin. They were no longer God-conscious or like God (Psalm 82:6). They became sin-conscious or carnal (being led by the senses) and decided to cover themselves and hide from God because of fear, guilt, and shame.

The story of the Garden of Eden says that satan talked to Eve and deceived her into eating the fruit. Yes, Eve was deceived, but Adam sinned or committed high treason because God gave the commandment to Adam. He had the authority and right to cast the snake (satan) out of the Garden of Eden, but Adam chose to believe what satan said about his identity. In Genesis 3:5 (KJV) says, *"For God doth know that in the day ye eat thereof, then your eyes shall be opened, and ye shall be as gods, knowing good and evil."* They were already like God because they were made in the image and likeness of Him. When you question your identity in God, it is easy to be tricked or persuaded to follow something false. As a result of sin entering the world through Adam's disobedience, God needed a ransom for mankind to be reconciled back to Him. Genesis 3:15 speaks about the coming of Jesus, a Savior, to reconcile us back to God, the Father.

Since the initial sin of the world, God, through history, has been moving us closer to reconciliation with him. However, sometimes, things seem to move in the wrong direction... For example... the story of Abraham having to sacrifice Isaac, his son, is symbolic of Jesus being the ransom for the entire world. God promised Abraham that he would be the father of many nations through his seed, Isaac. Now, God is asking Abraham to sacrifice his son. Abraham was willing to sacrifice Isaac because he held to God's covenant that was made with him in Genesis chapter 15. Because of Abraham's willingness to sacrifice Isaac, God knew that He had to sacrifice Jesus, His only Son. Abraham placed his total trust in God and believed that God would do the supernatural (raising Isaac from the dead), if necessary, because of His (God's) initial promise that He (God) called Abraham the father of many nations.

> It was by faith that Abraham offered Isaac as a sacrifice when God was testing him. Abraham, who had received God's promises, was ready to sacrifice his only son, Isaac, even though God had told him, "Isaac is the son through whom your descendants will be counted." Abraham reasoned that if Isaac died, God would be able to bring him back to life again. And in a sense, Abraham did receive his son back from the dead.

> **(Hebrews 11:17–19 NLT)**

CHAPTER 3

Betrayal

Betrayal is something Jesus knows about and experienced. In chapter 26 of Matthew, Jesus spoke of being betrayed several times. Judas Iscariot, a disciple of Jesus who fellowshipped with Him and was the treasurer, allowed the enemy to enter his heart (Luke 22:3). Judas knew that Jesus was a great man and was the Son of God. The unfortunate ending is the fact that he allowed greed or self-effort to become the center of his thoughts instead of continuing to keep his focus on Jesus.

Throughout the Bible, we read about the commandment to love God with all our hearts. Some places add that we are to love God with all our hearts, souls, and minds. The best way to understand the importance of working towards this goal is to illustrate the relationship God, the Father, had with Jesus while He walked the earth. On many occasions, Jesus said that He only spoke what the Father had Him to say, and He only did what the Father instructed Him to do (John 12:49, 14:10). The bond of love between them was extremely strong. When reading about the story of Jesus praying in the Garden of Gethsemane and as He prayed, His sweat was "...*as it were great drops of blood falling down to the ground*" (Luke 22:44 KJV), the agony Jesus was going through was concerning His separation from the Father and not so much the cross He was about to bear for the world. This is *"the perfect picture of love"*[6] and how much Jesus and God are One. However, Jesus knew that this separation was temporary and that God would once again have a right to His creation.

The betrayal of what Judas did was necessary to have us reconciled back to the Father, and Jesus was willing to separate Himself from the Father so we all would have a right to the Tree of Life. It was authentic, unconditional love that led Jesus to the cross to die for us. He was made sin for us. This was the only way He could be admitted into hell to obtain victory over sin. God "...*made Him [Jesus] to be sin for us, who knew no sin; that we might be made the righteousness of God in Him*" (2 Corinthians 5:21 KJV). Essentially, Jesus had to look like sin to free us from sin and become righteous or have right standing with God.

What does it mean to be betrayed? Synonyms for betrayal are *"unfaithfulness," "infidelity," "disloyal,"* and so on. These words lead one to think about someone being unfaithful outside of marriage or committing adultery. While this is true, there are other acts of betrayal to consider. For

6 Copeland and Copeland, 2012, p. 234.

instance, one's career. Is your focus more on advancing up the ladder of success in your company, where you tend to sacrifice a good number of nights away from home? While it is important to give your best at work, work must not become greater or more important than your spouse and certainly not God. You must reflect and recall the vows (promises) you made to your spouse. Do you recall the vows you said to your spouse? Make a checklist and see where you are. Are you on track and fulfilling what you vowed to do? Are you missing it somewhere? Have you changed your course or direction of the marriage, and your spouse is unaware of the change? Answering these questions and more will aid you in avoiding the road of betrayal, or if you went down that road, these questions will help you define where you are and what you need to do to get back on the right road.

Busyness can be dangerous when it is not put in proper perspective. Examples of busyness may include being heavily involved in school activities, working in the community, attending family outings, participating in and volunteering for church activities/commitments, job responsibilities, and the like. While these things are not wrong, they must not take God's time, your spouse's time, or other important times. Marriages are to be a mirror of your relationship with God Almighty. Do you only talk to God in the morning and then right before you go to bed? What relationship is that? Spending time continuously throughout the day is what God desires. Communing and consulting God in everything is the ultimate of walking by faith and not by sight (2 Corinthians 5:7) and trusting God with your whole heart to allow Him to direct your paths (Proverbs 3:5–6).

In married living, if we are not careful, we will fall into similar traps the enemy sets. The focus must be on the marriage by keeping God in the center of the marriage and allowing Him to direct our ways on how to treat our spouse, children, and others. When the attention is no longer on keeping the marriage unified by keeping God in the center, self-centeredness will show up, and more than likely, a great fall may take place. In essence, betrayal takes precedence instead of commitment or unification. When betrayal is present, what is the solution?

In the book *Vengeance of the Lord: The Justice System of God*, Dr. Bill Winston shares the importance of not seeking revenge when someone wrongs you. It is important to allow God to handle the betrayal. Our job is to trust God and rest in Him. We should not be in a state to retaliate because that is revenge and not vengeance.

Vengeance is not revenge. Revenge is a

principle of the kingdom of darkness, along with hatred, witchcraft, division, greed, threats, and so on. They all bring destruction. As Galatians 5:21 AMP says, *those who practice such things will not inherit the kingdom of God.* For the believer, God fights our battles.[7]

Therefore, it is important and necessary that we forgive the betrayal and allow God to do the rest. In an article by Dr. Frederick DiBlasio, he presents information from a cognitive behavioral approach that forgiveness is decision-based and not an emotion or feeling. Dr. DiBlasio states:

> Decision-based forgiveness is defined as the cognitive letting go of resentment, bitterness, and need for vengeance. By this definition, emotional readiness is not a factor in the decision process. There is a separation of reason from feelings in making the forgiveness decision, followed by an act of will. Consequently, people can choose to forgive or not to forgive. This approach is consistent with cognitive-behavioral approaches to therapy.[8]

---

7 Bill Winston, *Vengeance of the* Lord (Oak Park: Bill Winston Ministries, 2019), p. 66.
8 Frederick Diblasio, "Decision-Based Forgiveness Treatment in Cases of Marital Infidelity," *Psychotherapy: Theory, Research, Practice, Training* 37, no. 2 (July 1, 2000): 150, https://doi.org/10.1037/h0087834.

According to Dr. DiBlasio, research and reports show that when you release the decision to forgive, the existence of negative emotions surrounding the behavior dissipates. Essentially, you take command over your emotions and allow the Holy Spirit to heal. Colossians 3:12–15 (NLT) tells us the results of forgiveness.

> Since God chose you to be the holy people he loves, you must clothe yourselves with tenderhearted mercy, kindness, humility, gentleness, and patience. Make allowance for each other's faults and forgive anyone who offends you. Remember, the Lord forgave you, so you must forgive others. Above all, clothe yourselves with love, which binds us all together in perfect harmony. And let the peace that comes from Christ rule in your hearts. For as members of one body, you are called to live in peace. And always be thankful.

Immediate forgiveness keeps the airways open to hearing from God. You have the enemy under your feet because you are not yielding to the negative thoughts and actions he conjures up in your thoughts. To the world, this immediate forgiveness sounds crazy or immature. The truth of the matter is that harboring unforgiveness becomes the driving force, and that is immaturity. The person who chooses not to forgive becomes a slave to that offense. Research shows that unforgiveness is bondage that may lead to health issues that are serious and sometimes deadly.[9]

Betrayal is certainly an issue where one may say or believe that forgiving is impossible. As the Scripture states, *"With man this is impossible, but with God all things are possible"* (Matthew 19:26 (NIV); Mark 10:27; Luke 1:37). In short, overcoming the hurt or act of betrayal is to walk in love. Choosing or deciding to operate in unconditional love instead of self-centeredness becomes the pathway to mending the broken relationship and starting the rebuilding process of trust and hopefulness toward wholeness and maturity.

---

9 Diblasio, 2000.

CHAPTER 4

Supernatural vs. Natural

The Apostle Paul encourages the Church of Ephesus to be strong in God's might and power (Ephesians 6:10–18). He tells them that success or victory against the attacks or strategies of the enemy only comes when resting and relying on the Word of God and His promises.

> In conclusion be strong—not in yourselves but in the Lord, in the power of his boundless resource. Put on God's complete armour so that you can successfully resist all the devil's methods of attack. For our fight is not against any physical enemy: it is against organisations and powers that are spiritual. We are up against the unseen power that controls this dark world, and spiritual agents from the very headquarters of evil. Therefore, you must wear the whole armour of God that you may be able to resist evil in its day of power, and that even when you have fought to a standstill you may still stand your ground. Take your stand then with truth as your belt,

righteousness your breastplate, the Gospel
of peace firmly on your feet, salvation as
your helmet and in your hand the sword of
the Spirit, the Word of God. Above all be
sure you take faith as your shield, for it can
quench every burning missile the enemy
hurls at you. Pray at all times with every
kind of spiritual prayer, keeping alert and
persistent as you pray for all Christ's men
and women.

(PHILLIPS)

I also appreciate the *Message* translation. It gives a
more succinct picture of how believers are to fight when
attacked by the enemy. Following the steps in both translations guarantees victory.

And that about wraps it up. God is strong,
and he wants you strong. So take everything the Master has set out for you, well-
made weapons of the best materials. And
put them to use so you will be able to stand
up to everything the Devil throws your
way. This is no weekend war that we'll walk
away from and forget about in a couple
of hours. This is for keeps, a life-or-death
fight to the finish against the Devil and all
his angels. Be prepared. You're up against

far more than you can handle on your own. Take all the help you can get, every weapon God has issued, so that when it's all over but the shouting you'll still be on your feet. Truth, righteousness, peace, faith, and salvation are more than words. Learn how to apply them. You'll need them throughout your life. God's Word is an *indispensable* weapon. In the same way, prayer is essential in this ongoing warfare. Pray hard and long. Pray for your brothers and sisters. Keep your eyes open. Keep each other's spirits up so that no one falls behind or drops out.

We must take advantage of every weapon of protection God has for us. As believers, we must realize that the enemy is too powerful for us to fight him from a natural standpoint (2 Corinthians 4:4). We must use supernatural powers to overcome the forces of the enemy, and we accomplish these attacks through the finished works of Jesus (John 16:33; 1 John 4:4, 5:4). Jesus gave us the ability to overcome the enemy by speaking words of faith and believing what we say will come to pass. We also must make certain our love walk is pure. Faith in the Word of God and walking in agape or unconditional love go hand in hand. To be victorious in defeating the attacks of the enemy, we must ensure that we are not harboring any unforgiveness, strife, hatred, or any such thing. To believe God's Word to work in our lives, we must have His love residing in our hearts.

The Word of God tells us that the enemy will come against us and work hard to get us out of love. He knows that when we walk in love, we defeat the fiery darts and all evil tricks or strategies the enemy tries to bring our way. The package that the enemy tempts us with is not something we have to accept. We must speak out loud and confess that we will not walk out of love. Say this, "I choose to walk in love, always." Now, understand there may be times when we miss the mark and walk in selfishness. When we miss the mark, we must repent and receive God's forgiveness. Therefore, making the declaration continuously to walk in love because walking in love is a choice, the times we miss the mark will become less and less.

The Word of God will keep and protect us from yielding to the enemy's traps and tactics. Romans 12:2 reminds us that conforming to the ways of the world will not bring victory into our lives. Victory comes by transforming or renewing our minds (will, emotion, intellect, imagination). We accomplish this renewal by reading, studying, believing, hearing, and acting on the Word of God. When we choose to renew our soul (mind, will, emotion, intellect, and imagination), we are learning the perfect will God has for us. God has a purpose for each of us to fulfill on this earth, and the only way to complete the assignment is to learn from Him (God) the perfect and acceptable will He has for each of us.

When we confess the Word of God, we put it out in the atmosphere and allow the Word to operate on our behalf. We must speak the Word of God and not just think about God's Word when fighting the snares and attacks of the enemy. Indeed, we cannot fight thoughts with thoughts. We cannot stop thoughts (good or bad) from entering our minds. What we do once they enter our minds determines our destiny. Are we going to entertain or dismiss the thoughts? If they are good thoughts, begin to see if the thoughts are something God wants you to act on or if they are for pondering.

In Luke 2, the shepherds began to share with Mary and Joseph what the angel told them concerning Jesus. The Scripture says, *"And all they that heard it wondered at those things which were told them by the shepherds. But Mary kept all these things, and pondered them in her heart"* (Luke 2:18–19 KJV). Mary kept the sayings in her heart and thought often about what was said. She meditated on the words from the shepherds concerning Jesus. I believe this is why Mary was so confident to tell the servants at the wedding to do whatever Jesus said (John 2:1–11). This is an illustration of what we need to do when faced with adversity. We must often ponder or meditate on the Word of God. Joshua 1:8 tells us to meditate day and night. When we do this, we make our way prosperous, and we will have success.

Please understand that success is not having money, nice homes, luxury cars, or a good job. These things may be by-products of success. Success is nothing missing, lacking, or broken in your life. Success is wholeness: spirit, soul, and body. In 3 John 1:2 (KJV), it says, *"Beloved, I wish [or pray] above all things that thou mayest prosper and be in health, even as thy soul prospereth."* When you take God's Word and believe with all your heart that what He promised will come to pass, you will have success. The key is to meditate on His Word (day and night). Meditation brings revelation. As you sow the Word of God into your spirit man (Mark 4:14), the Word becomes alive, and revelation stirs up your imagination to bring forth good fruit, *"...some thirtyfold, some sixty, and some a hundred"* (Mark 4:20 KJV).

CHAPTER 5

Never-Ending Unfailing Love

Surely He has borne our griefs (sicknesses, weaknesses, and distresses) and carried our sorrows *and* pains [of punishment], yet we [ignorantly] considered Him stricken, smitten, and afflicted by God [as if with leprosy]. But He was wounded for our transgressions, He was bruised for our guilt *and* iniquities; the chastisement [needful to obtain] peace *and* well-being for us was upon Him, and with the stripes [that wounded] Him we are healed *and* made whole.

(Isaiah 53:4–5, AMPC)

Psalm 68:19 (KJV) says, *"Blessed be the Lord, who daily loadeth us with benefits, even the God of our salvation. Selah."* God is someone who delights in caring for us no matter what. He longs to do so much for us that He gave Jesus (His only Son) to take on the sins of the world to reconcile us back to Him.[10] Just think about that. Jesus, who was in Heaven enjoying daily fellowship with His Father

10 Copeland and Copeland, 2012, p. 300.

39

(face to face) and all the amenities, agreed to become the sacrificial Lamb so that we may experience the abundant, never-ending, unfailing love of God.

In 2 Corinthians 8:9, it tells us that Jesus, though He was rich, became poor so we may become rich. First, poor is relative. The riches and wealth Jesus has in Heaven are nothing compared to the riches or wealthiest person in this world. For instance, Revelation tells us that "...*the street of the city was pure gold, as it were transparent glass*" (Revelation 21:21b KJV). Therefore, since Jesus decided to come to earth and leave His wealth so that we may become wealthy, we must do the same—make the decision to love. Only when we allow God's love in our hearts that is given to us by the Holy Spirit (Romans 5:5) will we experience the true wealth and riches from God, Himself. Essentially, the key to wealth and riches is walking out the love designed by God.

> We are of God: he that knoweth God
> heareth us; he that is not of God heareth
> not us. Hereby know we the spirit of truth,
> and the spirit of error. Beloved, let us love
> one another: for love is of God; and ev-
> ery one that loveth is born of God, and
> knoweth God. He that loveth not knoweth
> not God; for God is love.

(1 John 4:6–8 KJV)

Living a life of love lets us know that sin cannot reign or have dominion in us (Romans 6:14). This is talking about the nature of sin. Once we accept Jesus as our Lord and Savior, sin is no longer in us (our spirit). This does not mean that we are perfect. It simply means we now have someone (the Holy Spirit) to lead, guide, and direct our paths. Living a "sin-free life" means we are not sin-conscious but God-conscious. We choose to walk in the love God established. We allow the love of God to be the center of our lives. When God's love becomes the center, we are walking and living a selfless life instead of a selfish life because sin is selfish. Sin is all about satisfying the self as opposed to walking in the love of God and depending on Him to lead, guide, and direct our paths.

What happens when we are sin-conscious? In the *Limitless Love* devotion, Brother Copeland states, *"We judge our inward capacity by our outward behavior, and we put more faith in our fleshly weaknesses than we do in THE WORD of God."*[11] Simply put, we must allow the Word of God and the Holy Spirit to cleanse us from our unrighteous thinking, which will, in turn, cleanse us from our unrighteous behavior. Romans 12:2 commands us to be transformed by the renewing of our minds. The only way to transform from sin consciousness to God consciousness

---

11 Copeland and Copeland, 2012, p. 245.

is by continuously renewing our minds with God's way of doing things.

In the Scripture, where Paul was bitten by a snake, the people who witnessed the act looked at Paul, waiting for him to die. They knew the snake was poisonous and believed the next step was death. The people knew the poison would soon spread through his body and kill him (Acts 28:3–6).

Taking this same incident and putting it in today's light of things, how often do we hear something and become one of the spreaders? Essentially, how many of us decide to gossip instead of shaking off the information or praying for our fellow believers who may have fallen? We see in the Scriptures that the people stood and waited for Paul to drop dead after the snake bit him. How often do we stand and wait for someone to become our garbage disposal, or how many times are we the garbage disposal?

We should become like Paul. When poison tries to enter, we should shake it off and maintain focus on God. We must continue to saturate ourselves with the Word of God and only speak what God says. This only comes through the continuous renewal of the mind. So, when the enemy tries to bring thoughts to our minds, we do not have to entertain them. We can examine those thoughts and ask if they are good and acceptable to God. If not, then we must do as Paul did with the poisonous snake—shake it off in the fire.

Entertaining rumors or participating in the art of gossiping contaminate one's ability to maintain a life of unconditional love. When the focus is on the person's wrongdoing or behavioral act, the love of God cannot and will not flow freely.

CHAPTER 6

The Good Shepherd

I am the good shepherd: the good shepherd giveth his life for the sheep. But he that is an hireling, and not the shepherd, whose own the sheep are not, seeth the wolf coming, and leaveth the sheep, and fleeth: and the wolf catcheth them, and scattereth the sheep. The hireling fleeth, because he is an hireling, and careth not for the sheep. I am the good shepherd, and know my sheep, and am known of mine. As the Father knoweth me, even so know I the Father: and I lay down my life for the sheep. And other sheep I have, which are not of this fold: them also I must bring, and they shall hear my voice; and there shall be one fold, and one shepherd. Therefore doth my Father love me, because I lay down my life, that I might take it again. No man taketh it from me, but I lay it down of myself. I have power to lay it down, and I have power to take it again. This commandment have I received of my Father.

(John 10:11–18 KJV)

In the devotion *Limitless Love*, Brother Copeland shares his thoughts on how great God's love is towards us and what He did to bring us back to Him.[12] *"Greater love has no one than this, than to lay down one's life for his friends"* (John 15:13 NKJV). This passage of scripture describes Jesus as the Good Shepherd and His willingness to give His life for us on the cross to reconcile us back to God. This is indeed an awesome picture of unconditional love, and yet the love of God goes deeper than the death, burial, and resurrection acts of Jesus. It was Jesus who decided to become a human and experience all that we go through (hunger, temptations, tiredness, anger) and yet do no sin as a result. Because of His love for the Father and God's love for us (the world), Jesus chose to become the Son of Man. He left harmony, joy, and peace to reside in a sin-infested world full of hatred, chaos, disharmony, murder, robbery, and other types of violence and unclean spirits. Unconditional love led Jesus to become the Son of Man, forever because Hebrews 7:23–25 (MSG) tells us,

> Earlier there were a lot of priests, for they died and had to be replaced. But Jesus' priesthood is permanent. He's there from now to eternity to save everyone who comes to God through him, always on the job to speak up for them.

---

12 Copeland and Copeland, 2012, p. 275.

In the world, satisfaction usually comes when one succeeds or reaches a certain goal in life: job, family, monetary status, education, and the like. These are all self-gratification or self-centered goals. However, as a believer, the most gratification or satisfaction received is when compassion or goodness is demonstrated to others as the Holy Spirit leads. Operating in the compassion of love under the prompting of the Holy Spirit is God's love flowing through a believer to reach people in need. When we allow the Holy Spirit to guide our thinking, we allow good nourishment to strengthen and build up our inner man. Now, we are exemplifying the *Good Shepherd*, the greatest love ever known.[13]

13 Copeland and Copeland, 2012, p. 259.

CHAPTER 7

Psalm 23

So often, Psalm 23 is used when persons are buried, or their bodies are committed back to the earth to comfort the family during their time of bereavement or grief. This Psalm is more powerful than consoling families in their time of grief. Let us dissect each verse to open some revelation and powerful words David used to describe the goodness, faithfulness, and forever loving God.

> The LORD is my shepherd; I have all that
> I need. He lets me rest in green meadows;
> he leads me beside peaceful streams. He
> renews my strength. He guides me along
> right paths, bringing honor to his name.
> Even when I walk through the darkest
> valley, I will not be afraid, for you are close
> beside me. Your rod and your staff protect
> and comfort me. You prepare a feast for me
> in the presence of my enemies. You hon-
> or me by anointing my head with oil. My
> cup overflows with blessings. Surely your
> goodness and unfailing love will pursue me

all the days of my life, and I will live in the house of the LORD forever.

(NLT)

Verse 1: "The Lord is my shepherd; I have all I need."

This verse tells me that everything I need comes from the Lord because He was the One willing to sacrifice His life for me. As noted in the previous chapter, John 10:11 (NLT) says, *"I am the Good Shepherd. The Good Shepherd sacrifices His life for the sheep."* Essentially, all I need (life, health, finances, emotional stability, mental soundness) is in Jesus. Therefore, my striving to get or obtain something is counterproductive because Jesus has already acquired all I need. My job is to maintain what Jesus obtained.

I am reminded of the parable of the Prodigal Son. There was a father who had two sons. So often, messages point to the demand the younger son made to his father about receiving his inheritance. The younger son did not want to wait for his inheritance. He wanted it immediately. According to the story, the father divided the inheritance between the two sons, and not long after the younger son received his inheritance, he left and resided in a faraway country. Being undisciplined, the younger son wasted his money, and soon a famine came through that country.

As the story goes, the son came to himself and realized what he had left. He decided to go back home, ask for forgiveness, and ask his father to allow him to be a servant. The story says that when the father saw the son a long way off, he [the father] went to greet him. The son began his speech by asking for forgiveness and requesting that he become a servant. The father chose not to listen and decided to celebrate his homecoming. The older son, who was in the field, heard the celebratory music in honor of his brother's return and became jealous. He would not participate in the celebration of his brother's welcome home party. The father came out to convince the older son to join the party, but the older son refused and said,

"All these years I've slaved for you and
never once refused to do a single thing you
told me to. And in all that time you never
gave me even one young goat for a feast
with my friends. Yet when this son of yours
comes back after squandering your money on prostitutes, you celebrate by killing
the fattened calf!" His father said to him,
"Look, dear son, you have always stayed by
me, and everything I have is yours. We had
to celebrate this happy day. For your broth-

er was dead and has come back to life! He was lost, but now he is found!"

(Luke 15:29–32 NLT)

The emphasis I would like to make is when the father said, *"Everything I have is yours."* You see, neither son needed to ask or seek anything because the father had already provided all they needed. The older son did not realize he could have a party for his friends anytime he wanted. He did not see himself as a son. He saw himself as a servant because the Scripture said he was in the field. Although he did not leave his father, he did not see himself as an owner or operating in a lordship capacity.

While the younger son took advantage of demanding his portion, he was not mature enough to handle the riches given to him because he was disconnected from his father. His immaturity and lack of discipline caused him to live a riotous lifestyle that ended in destruction.

You had wandered away like sheep. Now you have returned to the one who is your shepherd and protector.

(1 Peter 2:25 CEV)

In the Message translation, the Scripture says,

You were lost sheep with no idea who you were or where you were going. Now you're named and kept for good by the Shepherd of your souls.

(1 Peter 2:25 MSG)

In both cases, the sons need to recognize that their prosperity, success, growth, and sustainability stem from staying connected to their father. When remaining connected to their father, they have all (John 15:1–7). They need to take on the mindset of walking in the realm of ownership or lordship. Essentially, if the two sons mimic their father (Ephesians 5:1), they would realize they have all they need in the father who shepherds them. In other words, because the Lord is my source, I have everything I need.

Verse 2: "He lets me rest in green meadows; He leads me beside peaceful streams."

For me to rest peacefully in life, I must first cast my care or give all my worries over to God. He cares for me and will handle my situations if I trust and rest in Him (1 Peter 5:7; Hebrews 4:11). God wants me to rest and trust Him to orchestrate my life. The struggle happens when I try to take the lead. Now, I am working against the plans

God established. When I take the lead, I am saying that I do not trust God or I do not believe He has my best interest.

Psalm 1:1–3 (NLT) says,

> Oh, the joys of those who do not follow the advice of the wicked, or stand around with sinners, or join in with mockers. But they delight in the law of the LORD, meditating on it day and night. They are like trees planted along the riverbank, bearing fruit each season. Their leaves never wither, and they prosper in all they do.

> In addition, Matthew 11:28–30 (MSG) states, "Are you tired? Worn out? Burned out on religion? Come to me. Get away with me and you'll recover your life. I'll show you how to take a real rest. Walk with me and work with me—watch how I do it. Learn the unforced rhythms of grace. I won't lay anything heavy or ill-fitting on you. Keep company with me and you'll learn to live freely and lightly."

To rest in the peace of God that passes all understanding, I must learn to lean and depend on Him. I must trust God by relying on the Holy Spirit to guide me into all truths. The Holy Spirit is God's Spirit, so when I allow

Him (the Holy Spirit) to guide and direct my goings… I am genuinely trusting God. For indeed, it is God who is working in me to do His good pleasure (Philippians 2:13). My ways, thoughts, goings, and doings must be of the Lord. He will lead me down the right paths and never into a ditch (Isaiah 55:8; Proverbs 3:6).

Verse 3: "He renews my strength. He guides me along right paths, bringing honor to His name."

As I allow the Lord to direct my paths, my strength is renewed continuously. Isaiah 40:31 (NLT) says, *"But those who trust in the LORD will find new strength. They will soar high on wings like eagles. They will run and not grow weary. They will walk and not faint."* Putting my trust in God to direct my paths demonstrates how much I honor Him. God wants to give me all the benefits of being *one* of His. Psalm 103:5 (CEV) describes God's love for us, *"Each day that we live, He provides for our needs and gives us the strength of a young eagle."* The key to this strength is to lean and depend on His strength and trust His judgment. Each time I rely on God to lead and guide me, protection is guaranteed, and I am truly bringing honor to His name.

Whether the situation or circumstance is great or small, I must allow the Holy Spirit to get me to the finish line and not depend totally on my thought process or way of doing things. Relying on the Holy Spirit to get me to the finish line is called laboring to rest in the Word of God (Hebrews 4:11) and trusting Him to direct my paths (Proverbs 3:6). Self-centeredness does not bring honor to God's name. When I am walking in self-centeredness, I am using my strength and knowledge to get the job done. I am depending on my senses (touch, taste, sight, smell, and hearing). I am walking and operating in carnality. Thus, I make a concerted effort to keep God centered in all I do because when He is not in the center, I struggle, and chaos is inevitable.

Verse 4: "Even when I walk through the darkest valley, I will not be afraid, for you are close beside me. Your rod and your staff protect and comfort me."

The Scripture says that God promises to keep me in perfect peace as I keep my mind on Him and trust in Him. I will trust in the Lord because in Him is eternal strength (Isaiah 26:3–4). Because I know God will never leave or forsake me. I take comfort in knowing He is always with me, especially when things appear dark and dim. The key word in this verse is that whatever I encounter or face, I am going through it with God's help. He carries and takes me through the obstacles as long as I draw close to Him. Therefore, *"I will not be seized with alarm [I will not fear or dread or be terrified]. What can man do to me?"* (Hebrews 13:6b AMPC).

This type of assurance gives me the peace to rest. I know trials and tribulations will come, but because of Jesus, who overcame the world, I am an overcomer (John 16:33). I have the greater One in me, which makes me more than a conqueror. God says He will not leave me helpless, let me down, nor relax His hold on me. He always promises to be my *shelter*, *protector*, and *guide*. When I take my focus off me and rest in the finished works of Jesus, I am now moving from victory to victory and glory to glory. Going through a trial or tribulation is the necessary ingredient to maintain what Jesus obtained. Deciding to go through and rest on the promises of God's Word allows the Holy Spirit to do His job without my interference.

Verse 5: "You prepare a feast for me in the presence of my enemies. You honor me by anointing my head with oil. My cup overflows with blessings."

The love God has for me is so bold and strong that He dares to prepare a banquet feast before my enemies. He lets me know that He is my *protector* and *comforter*. He has me secured in His care. I am victorious when I believe and stand firm on the Word of God to deliver me no matter what. Hebrews 11:1 (AMPC) says,

"Now faith is the assurance (the confirmation, the title deed) of the things [we] hope

for, being the proof of things [we] do not
see *and* the conviction of their reality [faith
perceiving as real fact what is not revealed
to the senses]."

Many examples throughout the Bible illustrate the victory of faith in God, regardless of the obstacles or chal-
lenges presented. Joseph held on to his dream and became
Prime Minister of Egypt. He went from the pit to prison
to reigning in the palace, second to pharaoh. Each time
he faced adversity, the Scripture said, *"the Lord was with
Joseph"* (Genesis 39:2 NIV). Joseph's elevation to Prime
Minister helped his family, the people of Egypt, and all
other countries live in the overflow blessings (Genesis 41
and 42).

Another example of this verse five can be linked to the
story of Daniel in the lions' den (Daniel 6). Daniel knew
that God had his back when the decree went forth by King
Darius that no one was to pray to any God or man except to
the king for thirty days. If anyone is caught defying the decree, they will be thrown into the den of lions. The Scripture says that when Daniel knew the decree was signed, he
went to his living quarters and kneeled by his opened win-
dow to pray towards Jerusalem as he had done many times
before (Daniel 6:10). The leaders of the land were jealous

of Daniel because the king favored Daniel over the others.

As the story goes, the leaders went to the king to let him know that Daniel disobeyed the decree of the land. King Darius did not want to follow through with the punishment. However, being pressured by the leaders, King Darius had Daniel thrown into the den of lions. Early in the morning, King Darius arose to see if Daniel's God saved him from the mouths of the lions. God indeed saved Daniel from the mouths of the lions. Because the king perceived that he was tricked, he ordered the men (who tricked him) and their families to be thrown into the den of lions, and King Darius decreed to the people that Daniel's God was the true and living God.

Daniel honored God and did not back down from the written decree that went out. Instead, he chose to believe that God would deliver him in the presence of his enemies and cause his cup to overflow with blessings. Daniel changed the law of the land, which in turn blessed the people. Essentially, the *"Blessing"* that Daniel walked in affected the people of Persia. They became recipients of the *"Blessing"* because of Daniel.

Verse 6: "Surely your goodness and unfailing love will pursue me all the days of my life, and I will live in the house of the LORD forever."

God's unfailing and undying love pursues me each day. This speaks volumes. Who do you know that demonstrates unconditional love regardless of the response? Hebrews 13:5b (AMPC) says,

> for He [God] Himself has said, I will not in any way fail you nor give you up nor leave you without support. [I will] not, [I will] not, [I will] not in any degree leave you helpless nor forsake nor let [you] down (relax My hold on you)! [Assuredly not!]

God, through His Son, Jesus, made everything good available to us. All we need to do is receive and maintain the finished works Jesus obtained. To be successful and bathe in the goodness and unfailing love that God provides, we need to decide that we will abide in Jesus and allow Him (the Word of God) to abide in us. Our standard of living must be to reside in the Word of God forever.

CHAPTER 8

The Love Chapter (1 Corinthians 13)

Love endures long *and* is patient and kind;
love never is envious *nor* boils over with
jealousy, is not boastful *or* vainglorious,
does not display itself haughtily. It is not
conceited (arrogant and inflated with
pride); it is not rude (unmannerly) *and*
does not act unbecomingly. Love (God's
love in us) does not insist on its own rights
or its own way, *for* it is not self-seeking; it
is not touchy *or* fretful *or* resentful; it takes
no account of the evil done to it [it pays no
attention to a suffered wrong]. It does not
rejoice at injustice *and* unrighteousness,
but rejoices when right *and* truth prevail.
Love bears up under anything *and* everything that comes, is ever ready to believe
the best of every person, its hopes are fade-
less under all circumstances, and it endures
everything [without weakening]. Love
never fails [never fades out or becomes
obsolete or comes to an end].

(1 Corinthians 13:4–8a AMPC)

Why do I call this chapter *The Love Chapter*? These verses, inspired by Paul under the prompting of the Holy Spirit to write to the Church of Corinth, describe in detail the attributes and characteristics of our God. As believers, it should be our goal to aspire to imitate our Father, as recorded in Ephesians 5:1–2 (AMPC).

> Therefore be imitators of God [copy Him and follow His example], as well-beloved children [imitate their father]. And walk in love, [esteeming and delighting in one another] as Christ loved us and gave Himself up for us, a slain offering and sacrifice to God [for you, so that it became] a sweet fragrance.

Our relationship with one another should reflect our relationship with God, the Father. We should be forgiving and desire the best for others, especially our spouse, children, family members, friends, and yes, even our enemies. Colossians 3:13–14 instructs us to forgive one another as Christ forgave us. *"Forgive as quickly and completely as the Master forgave you. And regardless of what else you put on, wear love. It's your basic, all-purpose garment. Never be without it"* (MSG). As stated here, we are to forgive quickly and not dwell or meditate on what has been done to us. We must not become like the world. We must represent and show the love of God to the world. The only way to accomplish this directive is to imitate God. Essentially, if we choose not to exemplify the God kind of love (agape love), we are bankrupted. We are broke.

In the devotion from *Limitless Love*, Brother Copeland speaks about the love walk each Christian should exemplify because of God's love for us, according to 1 Corinthians 13.[14] This passage teaches us about the nature of God and how much He loves us. God does not keep score when we are in the wrong, nor does He become resentful. God's nature is love, and it is unconditional. He does not demand us to love Him, and He is not rude or discourteous when we choose not to reciprocate love towards Him. It is God's desire that we love with His love and do the right thing. God knows that doing right will help us grow closer to Him, and His nature will exude out of us more. God is the One who meets our needs. His love for us is so strong that He designed a great life for each of us. Every believer has an important role in enhancing the kingdom of God. However, God will not force His plans on us. We must be willing to allow God to direct our paths. He is the *ultimate gentleman*.

As stated by Brother Copeland from another devotion in the *Limitless Love*, we are responsible for how we treat

---

14 Copeland and Copeland, 2012, p. 141.

others, not how they treat us.[15] In the world, people would say this is crazy and unacceptable. However, the Scripture commands us to do to others as we would want them to do us (Luke 6:31). We must be willing to love, give, and do good to people no matter how they treat us. We must exemplify this God kind of love and expect nothing in return.

> "If you love only those who love you, why should you get credit for that? Even sinners love those who love them! And if you do good only to those who do good to you, why should you get credit? Even sinners do that much! And if you lend money only to those who can repay you, why should you get credit? Even sinners will lend to other sinners for a full return. "Love your enemies! Do good to them. Lend to them without expecting to be repaid. Then your reward from heaven will be very great, and you will truly be acting as children of the Most High, for he is kind to those who are unthankful and wicked. You must be compassionate, just as your Father is compassionate.

> **(Luke 6:32–36 NLT)**

Essentially, when we show the love of God despite the

---

15 Ibid, p. 112.

bigotry, animosity, or hatred directed at us, we triumph. Know this: a child of God standing in faith and walking in *"The Blessing"* will triumph and rule every time. The key is to keep your focus on the Word of God, walk in love, and choose not to be offended.

Furthermore, Brother Copeland shares the importance of giving one's way into love from the story of the rich young ruler and how giving equates with love.[16] The story of the rich young ruler in Mark chapter 10 teaches about trust and love. These two go hand in hand. If you trust something, you will love what you trust and do all you can to keep it. In the story, the rich young ruler asks Jesus what he must do to inherit eternal life (Mark 10:17). Jesus tells the young man to sell whatever he has and give to the poor. Up to this point, the young man was proud when he shared that he kept the commandments: *"...Do not commit adultery, Do not kill, Do not steal, Do not bear false witness, Defraud not, Honour thy father and mother"* (Mark 10:19 KJV). However, Jesus, in a loving manner, let him know that his trust was not in God but in his riches because when he told the young man to sell his riches and give to the poor, the rich young ruler went away sad. The Scripture says he had great possessions. Essentially, the possessions or riches had him. The rich young ruler loved his riches,

---

16 Copeland and Copeland, 2012, p. 144.

and his trust was in wealth and not in God.

We must put our trust in God and believe He will provide and take care of our every need (Philippians 4:19). God loves us too much to have us go hungry or not meet all our needs. He is a good and loving God. For this reason, we must imitate and copy God, who is our Father, and act like He acts (Ephesians 5:1). We see someone in need, and God directs us to give (time, money, encouragement, etc.); we must do it with a glad heart. We honor God's request and give because we trust Him to take care of us. When God instructs us to give or do something out of the norm, He wants us to step out of our comfort zone and trust Him. This is how we walk in *"The Blessing"*.

CHAPTER 9

What Does It Mean to Be Committed?

Do not love the world nor the things in the
world. If anyone loves the world, the love
of the Father is not in him. For all that is in
the world, the lust of the flesh and the lust
of the eyes and the boastful pride of life, is
not from the Father, but is from the world.
The world is passing away and *also* its lusts;
but the one who does the will of God con-
tinues *to live* forever.

(1 John 2:15–17 NASB)

In 1 John 2:15–17, it commands us not to love or put
our trust in the world. Yes, we are in the world, but we are
not of the world, and we should not resemble the world.
All the world has to offer are lustful things, and they are
temporary. We must recognize where our trust lies. If we
trust or lust after the things of the world, we are not relying on the Father or the Holy Spirit to help us. Essentially,
do you want temporary satisfaction or eternal life? *"While
we look not at the things which are seen, but at the things
which are not seen: for the things which are seen are tem-*

poral; but the things which are not seen are eternal" (2 Corinthians 4:18 KJV).

In the *Limitless Love* devotion, Brother Kenneth Copeland shares a story about a chicken and a pig going to a church prayer breakfast.[17] They asked the chicken to provide the eggs and the pig to provide the bacon. The pig turned to the chicken and said, "Miss Chicken, you are certainly involved, but I'm committed!"[18] As believers and followers of Christ, we must be involved and committed to exemplifying the love of God everywhere. There will be times we must give of ourselves and lay aside our wants and needs to focus on others. Often, when we get the attention off our wants and desires and allow the Holy Spirit to guide us to minister to others, our needs are met because God promises to provide for us (Philippians 4:19; Matthew 6:33). As we continue this act of giving, we are continuing the economic system of love. God gives to us, we give to others, God gives to us again, and so on.

It is a decision and not a feeling to commit to walking in love. What does that mean, and how can it be done? From a marital perspective, I extracted some strategies from Dr. Gary Chapman's book *Four Seasons of Marriage*[19] and

---

17 Copeland and Copeland, 2012, p. 176.
18 Ibid.
19 Gary Chapman, *The Four Seasons of Marriage: Secrets to a Lasting Marriage* (Carol Stream: Tyndale House Publishers, 2005), https://store.iblp.org/the-four-seasons-of-marriage-softcover.html.

Pastor Jimmy Evans' book *Marriage on the Rock,*[20] and I incorporated my views from the Word of God concerning *what* and *how to walk in* love:

What?

- We are to strive to walk continuously in agape love, regardless of the circumstance or situation.[21] Our love must be genuine (mirror the love God gave us in—John 3:16).

- Our words and actions need to be motivated by love (unconditional, agape love).

How?

- How can we be sure we haven't slipped into selfishness or self-centeredness? By keeping a close check on our joy level.[22]

- In John 15:10–11, Jesus said that He gave us the commandment of love so that His joy would remain in us, and our joy would be full. So, we can be sure if we're not experiencing joy, we're not walking in genuine love.[23]

- This is a decision we make regularly. In marriages,

20 Jimmy Evans, Marriage on the Rock: God's Design for Your Dream Marriage (Majestic Media, 1996)
21 Chapman, 2005.
22 Ibid.
23 Copeland and Copeland, 2012.

we tend to keep records of the things that hurt or make us not want to be around our spouse. When someone asks, "How's your spouse?" Does your mind trail to unpleasant things while saying, fine or doing well? Our joy level can remain full by seeing the value and good things in our spouse. We tend to major in the wrong areas.[24]

- Yes, bring things to the attention of your spouse, but do not dwell on or keep long records of wrong behavior. Keeping these records inhibits your growth in the Lord and the growth of the marriage.

- God said, *"For I will be merciful to their unrigh-teousness, and their sins and their iniquities I will remember no more"* (Hebrews 8:12 (KJV); 10:17). Because we have the Spirit of God in us, we must show His love and mercy not what we think they deserve because of the hurt.[25]

Explanation

- It is important to be happy with the service we give to others as well as the sacrifices the services may require. Producing or having a heaviness by in-wardly thinking with a heavy sigh, "I guess I must do this because it's the right thing. I'm not looking

24 Chapman, 2005.
25 Evans, 1996.

70

forward to it, but it's my duty, so I'll do it."[26]

- Remember, no one wants that kind of love. God doesn't want it, and neither does anyone else.

Solution

- If you ever catch yourself thinking that way, make a change. Get in the presence of the LORD. Worship and fellowship with Him until the genuine spirit of love comes alive in you again. Don't settle for superficial substitutes. [27]

- When it comes to love, make sure you have the real love that comes only from God.

- Remember, when you first loved your spouse, was your love genuine? If so, then reflect on what you did to maintain that genuine love and move in that direction. Our love for our spouses should mirror the relationship and love we have with God.

- NOTE: It is important to note that the same information (*What, How, Explanation, and Solution*) discussed above concerning marriage may be applied to any relationship.

The important thing to remember is that God yearns

---

26 Chapman, 2005; Evans, 1996.
27 Copeland and Copeland, 2012.

to communicate with us daily. He wants to have an intimate relationship with us. The intimacy God desires can be mirrored by a married couple getting to know one another each day. For married couples, true intimacy is not defined as something sexual or physical. The true physical aspects of intimacy with married couples come after the emotional and mental connection experience. With God, we are connected to Him spiritually first and then with our soul (mind, will, emotion, intellect, and imagination) as we purposefully renew it with His Word.

This is the battleground we normally fight with the enemy. The devil cannot penetrate or take control of our spirit man once we receive the Spirit of God into our spirit. We are now sealed with the Holy Spirit of promise because we believed (Ephesians 1:13). Therefore, we must act and renew our minds through the Word of God so that we will know God's way of thinking and doing things (Romans 12:2). This is what Gloria Copeland speaks about in the devotion about not being ready for the *woodpile*.[28] Satan will try all he can to present distractions, interruptions, and pressures to get us off course: praying, hearing God's Word preached, reading and studying God's Word, and fellowshipping with the Father.

These are some ways we learn God's character and na-

---

28 Copeland and Copeland, 2012, p. 292.

ture. This is how we become intimate with Him. Jesus said in John 15 that He is the true vine and God is the *husband-man* (*Gardener, Farmer, Vinedresser*). We are the branches connected to the *vine*. We will grow a great deal of fruit if we stay connected to the *vine* (see Chapter 7). In essence, commitment becomes a necessity and not an option.

CHAPTER 10

Remember the Benefits

God loves each of us so much that He gave His only Son to bring us back to Him (see John 3:16). Jesus died and was made "...sin for us, who knew no sin; that we might be made the righteousness of God..." (2 Corinthians 5:21 KJV). Jesus, as the last Adam (1 Corinthians 15:45), not only gave His life and reconciled us back to God but enabled us to inherit benefits because of Abraham (Galatians 3:13–14, 29). We are the seed of Abraham because of Jesus (His death, burial, resurrection, and ascension). The finished works of Jesus placed every born-again believer into the family of God and gave us access to everything originally given to the first Adam in the Garden of Eden. Therefore, we have the right not only to remember all the benefits Jesus provided, but we must also decree, declare, and accept these benefits in our lives. What are our benefits? Romans 14:17 (KJV) says, *"For the kingdom of God is not meat and drink; but righteousness, and peace, and joy in the Holy Ghost."* Below are two translations of Psalm 103:1–8 depicting our benefits.

Bless the Lord, O my soul; And all that is within me, *bless* His holy name! Bless the Lord, O my soul, And forget not all His benefits: Who forgives all your iniquities, Who heals all your diseases, Who redeems your life from destruction, Who crowns you with lovingkindness and tender mercies, Who satisfies your mouth with good *things, So that* your youth is renewed like the eagle's. The Lord executes righteousness And justice for all who are oppressed. He made known His ways to Moses, His acts to the children of Israel. The Lord *is* merciful and gracious, Slow to anger, and abounding in mercy.

(NKJV)

Let all that I am praise the Lord; with my whole heart, I will praise his holy name. Let all that I am praise the Lord; may I never forget the good things he does for me. He forgives all my sins and heals all my diseases. He redeems me from death and crowns me with love and tender mercies. He fills my life with good things. My youth is renewed like the eagle's! The Lord gives righteousness and justice to all who are treated unfairly. He revealed his char-

76

acter to Moses and his deeds to the people of Israel. The LORD is compassionate and merciful, slow to get angry and filled with unfailing love.

(NLT)

Once again, we see how infinite God loves us and wants to do so much for us. David, in this Psalm, shares how much God loves us. He describes the true character of God in these verses. We should honor, adore, extol, and exalt God all the days of our lives. Let us break down our need to bless God continuously. Verse three says, *"He forgives all my sins and heals all my diseases."* The finished works of Jesus eradicated our sins (past, present, and future).

The Scripture says that without the shed blood, there is no remission of sins (see Hebrews 9:22). Our focus no longer is on our behavior or what we need to do to be right with God. Our focus is to rest in the finished works of Jesus (Hebrew 4:11) and know that because of His finished works, we reap the benefits of salvation (Wholeness: nothing missing, broken, or lacking). This wholeness includes walking in divine health. We do not have to endure any disease or sickness the enemy may try to give us. Any package that the enemy brings, we do not have to accept the package. Jesus took care of all the evil and unclean works so that we could reap all the benefits.

Verse 4: *"He redeems me from death and crowns me with love and tender mercies."*

It was Jesus who transferred us from death to life because of His finished works on the cross. We were born and shaped in sin. This was our nature. Jesus, therefore, gave us the ticket to be reborn or born again by accepting and believing in His finished works. Romans 10:9 tells us that if we confess with our mouths the Lord Jesus and believe in our hearts that God raised Jesus from the dead, we are saved. Jesus became sin for us so that we can have life eternal, which includes love and the mercies of God.

Verse 5: *"He fills my life with good things. My youth is renewed like the eagle's!"*

The Apostle Paul tells us in Ephesians that we are to act like God, Our Father, and imitate Him (Ephesians 5:1). We can accomplish this because, as a believer, we have the nature of God in us. God is good, and He only wants the best for us. Therefore, we must decree and declare that "God only wants good for me. He does not want anything bad or hurtful to happen to me or my family. He is the One who fills my life with '*The Blessing*.'"

78

It is necessary that, as believers, we put our trust and belief in God to take care of us and provide us with good things. As we rest in His promises, we must not become anxious or worried about anything (Philippians 4:6). Like eagles, we are fearless and put our trust and security in Him (God). We know that God has our back and will never leave us. Simply put, we do not give up. We stand firm in our faith and trust God. *"Preserve me, O God: for in thee do I put my trust"* (Psalm 16:1 KJV).

Verses 6 and 7: *"The Lord gives righteousness and justice to all who are treated unfairly. He revealed his character to Moses and his deeds to the people of Israel."*

We must not retaliate or allow resentment to harbor or take residence in our spirits when treated unfairly. Resentment and *emotional retaliation* are negative responses that will lead you down the wrong path.[29] We must not allow our emotions to lead us. We must be led by the Spirit of God and allow Him to be our vindicator. As recorded in Romans 12:19 (KJV), *"Dearly beloved, avenge not yourselves, but rather give place unto wrath: for it is written, Vengeance is mine; I will repay, saith the Lord"* (also see Hebrews 10:30).

When we allow God to fight our battles, we are pro-

---

29 Winston, 2019.

tected. Psalm 91:4 (AMPC) tells us that *"He [God] will cover you with His pinions, and under His wings shall you trust and find refuge; His truth and His faithfulness are a shield and a buckler."* Therefore, "If vengeance is understood and believed, it guarantees the protection of your mind, your body and all that you have (family, material possessions, etc.)."[30]

Verse 8: *"The LORD is compassionate and merciful, slow to get angry and filled with unfailing love."*

This verse gives us a clear picture of God's character. He is merciful, compassionate, caring, and always abounding in love. In other words, despite our sins, mistakes, errors, and disappointments, God is always there to grant us mercy and not give us what we deserve. What a loving Father we have!

---

30 Winston, 2019, p. 67.

EPILOGUE

The love of God is simply God showing or displaying His goodness to us. He desires always to uplift and give us the best. At no time does God want us to fail or become entangled with the yoke of bondage (Galatians 5:1). This is why He sent Jesus, His dear Son, into the world not only to save us and bring us out of bondage but He wanted to show and share His goodness to us. God's plan for us is to be victorious in every area of our lives. Once we have accepted Jesus to become our Lord and Savior, we are whole: nothing missing, broken, or lacking. Everything we desire has already been done because of the finished works of Jesus. The love of God is His goodness shown towards us. The song: *Goodness of God* truly depicts the character and *unconditional love* God has for us.

GOODNESS OF GOD
I love You, Lord
For Your mercy never fails me
All my days, I've been held in Your hands
From the moment that I wake up
Until I lay my head
Oh, I will sing of the goodness of God

And all my life You have been faithful
And all my life You have been so, so good
With every breath that I am able
Oh, I will sing of the goodness of God

I love Your voice
You have led me through the fire
In the darkest night
You are close like no other
I've known You as a Father
I've known You as a Friend
And I have lived in the goodness of God
(yeah)

And all my life You have been faithful (oh)
And all my life You have been so, so good
With every breath that I am able
Oh, I will sing of the goodness of God
(yeah)

'Cause Your goodness is running after
It's running after me
Your goodness is running after
It's running after me
With my life laid down
I'm surrendered now
I give You everything
'Cause Your goodness is running after
It's running after me (oh-oh)

'Cause Your goodness is running after
It's running after me
Your goodness is running after
It's running after me
With my life laid down
I'm surrendered now
I give You everything[31]

---

31 "Bethel Music: Goodness Of God by Brian Johnson, Jason Ingram, Ed Cash, Ben Fielding, and Jenn Johnson," Azlyrics.com, 2019, https://www.azlyrics.com/lyrics/bethelmusic/goodnessofgod.html.

APPENDIX

Chapter 1: How Do I Know That God Loves Me?

We love him, because He first loved us.

(1 John 4:19 KJV)

And ye are complete in him, which is the head of all principality and power:

(Colossians 2:10 KJV)

...I came that they may have and enjoy life, and have it in abundance (to the full, till it overflows).

(John 10:10b AMPC)

And if children, then heirs; heirs of God, and joint-heirs with Christ; if so be that we suffer with him, that we may be also glorified together.

(Romans 8:17 KJV)

As for me, behold, my covenant is with thee, and thou shalt be a father of many nations. Neither shall thy name any more be called Abram, but thy name shall be Abraham; for a father of many nations have ⁻ made thee. And I will make thee exceeding fruitful, and I will make nations of thee, and kings shall come out of thee. And I will establish my covenant between me and thee and thy seed after thee in their generations for an everlasting covenant, to be a God unto thee, and to thy seed after thee.

(Genesis 17:4–7)

Chapter 2: What is the Difference? (Conditional Love vs. Unconditional Love)

If you were of the world, the world would love its own; but because you are not of the world, but I chose you out of the world, because of this the world hates you.

(John 15:19 NASB 1995)

I have given them Your word; and the world has hated them because they are not of the world, just as I am not of the world. I do not pray that You should take them out of the world, but that You should keep them from the evil one. They are not of the world, just as I am not of the world.

(John 17:14–16 NKJV)

If the world hate you, ye know that it hated me before it hated you. If ye were of the world, the world would love his own: but because ye are not of the world, but I have chosen you out of the world, therefore the world hateth you.

(John 15:18–19 KJV)

Now then we are ambassadors for Christ, as though God did beseech you by us: we pray you in Christ's stead, be ye reconciled to God.

(2 Corinthians 5:20 KJV)

Ye are the light of the world. A city that is set on an hill cannot be hid. Neither do men light a candle, and put it under a bushel, but on a candlestick; and it giveth light unto all that are in the house. Let your light so shine before men, that they may see your good works, and glorify your Father which is in heaven.

(Matthew 5:14–16 KJV)

But I say unto you which hear, Love your enemies, do good to them which hate you, Bless them that curse you, and pray for them which despitefully use you. And unto

him that smiteth thee on the one cheek
offer also the other; and him that taketh
away thy cloak forbid not to take thy coat
also. Give to every man that asketh of thee;
and of him that taketh away thy goods ask
them not again. And as ye would that men
should do to you, do ye also to them likewise. For if ye love them which love you,
what thank have ye? for sinners also love
those that love them. And if ye do good to
them which do good to you, what thank
have ye? for sinners also do even the same.
And if ye lend to them of whom ye hope
to receive, what thank have ye? for sinners
also lend to sinners, to receive as much
again. But love ye your enemies, and do
good, and lend, hoping for nothing again;
and your reward shall be great, and ye shall
be the children of the Highest: for he is
kind unto the unthankful and to the evil.
Be ye therefore merciful, as your Father
also is merciful.

(Luke 6:27–36 KJV)

That at that time ye were without Christ,
being aliens from the commonwealth of
Israel, and strangers from the covenants of
promise, having no hope, and without God

in the world: But now in Christ Jesus ye who sometimes were far off are made nigh by the blood of Christ. For he is our peace, who hath made both one, and hath broken down the middle wall of partition between us; Having abolished in his flesh the enmity, even the law of commandments contained in ordinances; for to make in himself of twain one new man, so making peace; And that he might reconcile both unto God in one body by the cross, having slain the enmity thereby: And came and preached peace to you which were afar off, and to them that were nigh. For through him we both have access by one Spirit unto the Father. Now therefore ye are no more strangers and foreigners, but fellowcitizens with the saints, and of the household of God;

(Ephesians 2:12–19 KJV)

Ye adulterers and adulteresses, know ye not that the friendship of the world is enmity with God? whosoever therefore will be a friend of the world is the enemy of God. Do ye think that the scripture saith in vain, The spirit that dwelleth in us lusteth to envy? But he giveth more grace. Where-

fore he saith, God resisteth the proud,
but giveth grace unto the humble. Submit
yourselves therefore to God. Resist the
devil, and he will flee from you.

(James 4:4–7 KJV)

For if ye love them which love you, what thank
have ye? for sinners also love those that love
them. And if ye do good to them which do
good to you, what thank have ye? for sinners
also do even the same. And if ye lend to them
of whom ye hope to receive, what thank have
ye? for sinners also lend to sinners, to receive
as much again.

(Luke 6:32–34 KJV)

According as he hath chosen us in him before
the foundation of the world, that we should be
holy and without blame before him in love:

(Ephesians 1:4 KJV)

And the Lord God said unto the woman, What
is this that thou hast done? And the woman
said, The serpent beguiled me, and I did eat.

(Genesis 3:13 KJV)

I have said, Ye are gods; and all of you are children of the most High.

(Psalm 82:6 KJV)

And I will put enmity between thee and the woman, and between thy seed and her seed; it shall bruise thy head, and thou shalt bruise his heel.

(Genesis 3:15 KJV)

Chapter 3: Betrayal

Then entered Satan into Judas surnamed Iscariot, being of the number of the twelve.

(Luke 22:3 KJV)

For I have not spoken of myself; but the Father which sent me, he gave me a commandment, what I should say, and what I should speak.

(John 12:49 KJV)

Believest thou not that I am in the Father, and the Father in me? the words that I speak unto you I speak not of myself: but the Father that dwelleth in me, he doeth the works.

(John 14:10 KJV)

Chapter 4: Supernatural vs. Natural

In whom the god of this world hath blind-
ed the minds of them which believe not,
lest the light of the glorious gospel of
Christ, who is the image of God, should
shine unto them.

(2 Corinthians 4:4 KJV)

These things I have spoken unto you, that
in me ye might have peace. In the world
ye shall have tribulation: but be of good
cheer; I have overcome the world.

(John 16:33 KJV)

Ye are of God, little children, and have
overcome them: because greater is he that
is in you, than he that is in the world.

(1 John 4:4 KJV)

For whatsoever is born of God overcometh
the world: and this is the victory that overcometh the world, even our faith.

(1 John 5:4 KJV)

And the third day there was a marriage in
Cana of Galilee; and the mother of Jesus

was there: And both Jesus was called, and his disciples, to the marriage. And when they wanted wine, the mother of Jesus saith unto him, They have no wine. Jesus saith unto her, Woman, what have I to do with thee? mine hour is not yet come. His mother saith unto the servants, Whatsoever he saith unto you, do it. And there were set there six waterpots of stone, after the manner of the purifying of the Jews, containing two or three firkins apiece. Jesus saith unto them, Fill the waterpots with water. And they filled them up to the brim. And he saith unto them, Draw out now, and bear unto the governor of the feast. And they bare it. When the ruler of the feast had tasted the water that was made wine, and knew not whence it was: (but the servants which drew the water knew;) the governor of the feast called the bridegroom, And saith unto him, Every man at the beginning doth set forth good wine; and when men have well drunk, then that which is worse: but thou hast kept the good wine until now. This beginning of miracles did Jesus in Cana of Galilee, and manifested forth his glory; and his disciples believed on him.

(John 2:1–11 KJV)

Chapter 5: Never-Ending Unfailing Love

And hope maketh not ashamed; because
the love of God is shed abroad in our
hearts by the Holy Ghost which is given
unto us.

(Romans 5:5 KJV)

For sin shall not have dominion over you:
for ye are not under the law, but under
grace.

(Romans 6:14 KJV)

And be not conformed to this world: but
be ye transformed by the renewing of your
mind, that ye may prove what is that good,
and acceptable, and perfect, will of God.

(Romans 12:2 KJV)

And when Paul had gathered a bundle
of sticks, and laid them on the fire, there
came a viper out of the heat, and fastened
on his hand. And when the barbarians
saw the venomous beast hang on his hand,
they said among themselves, No doubt this
man is a murderer, whom, though he hath
escaped the sea, yet vengeance suffereth
not to live. And he shook off the beast into

the fire, and felt no harm. Howbeit they looked when he should have swollen, or fallen down dead suddenly: but after they had looked a great while, and saw no harm come to him, they changed their minds, and said that he was a god.

(Acts 28:3–6 KJV)

Chapter 7: Psalm 23

I am the true vine, and my Father is the husbandman. Every branch in me that beareth not fruit he taketh away: and every branch that beareth fruit, he purgeth it, that it may bring forth more fruit. Now ye are clean through the word which I have spoken unto you. Abide in me, and I in you. As the branch cannot bear fruit of itself, except it abide in the vine; no more can ye, except ye abide in me. I am the vine, ye are the branches: He that abideth in me, and I in him, the same bringeth forth much fruit: for without me ye can do nothing. If a man abide not in me, he is cast forth as a branch, and is withered; and men gather them, and cast them into the fire, and they are burned. If ye abide in me, and my words abide in you,

ye shall ask what ye will, and it shall be
done unto you.

(John 15:1–7 KJV)

Therefore be imitators of God [copy Him
and follow His example], as well-beloved
children [imitate their father].

(Ephesians 5:1 AMPC)

Casting all your care upon him; for he
careth for you.

(1 Peter 5:7 KJV)

Let us labour therefore to enter into that
rest, lest any man fall after the same example of unbelief.

(Hebrews 4:11 KJV)

[Not in your own strength] for it is God
Who is all the while effectually at work in
you [energizing and creating in you the
power and desire], both to will and to work
for His good pleasure *and* satisfaction *and*
delight.

(Philippians 2:13 AMPC)

For my thoughts are not your thoughts,
neither are your ways my ways, saith the
Lord.

(Isaiah 55:8 KJV)

In all thy ways acknowledge him, and he
shall direct thy paths.

(Proverbs 3:6 KJV)

These things I have spoken unto you, that
in me ye might have peace. In the world
ye shall have tribulation: but be of good
cheer; I have overcome the world.

(John 16:33 KJV)

Now when Daniel knew that the writing
was signed, he went into his house; and his
windows being open in his chamber toward Jerusalem, he kneeled upon his knees
three times a day, and prayed, and gave
thanks before his God, as he did aforetime.

(Daniel 6:10 KJV)

Chapter 8: The Love Chapter (1 Corinthians 13)

And as ye would that men should do to
you, do ye also to them likewise.

(Luke 6:31 KJV)

And when he was gone forth into the way, there came one running, and kneeled to him, and asked him, Good Master, what shall I do that I may inherit eternal life?

(Mark 10:17 KJV)

Chapter 9: What Does It Mean to Be Committed?

For God so loved the world, that he gave his only begotten Son, that whosoever believeth in him should not perish, but have everlasting life.

(John 3:16 KJV)

But my God shall supply all your need according to his riches in glory by Christ Jesus.

(Philippians 4:19 KJV)

But seek ye first the kingdom of God, and his righteousness; and all these things shall be added unto you.

(Matthew 6:33 KJV)

If ye keep my commandments, ye shall abide in my love; even as I have kept my Father's commandments, and abide in his love. These things have I spoken unto you, that my joy might remain in you, and that your joy might be full.

(John 15:10–11 KJV)

For I will be merciful to their unrighteousness, and their sins and their iniquities will I remember no more.

(Hebrews 8:12 KJV)

And their sins and iniquities will I remember no more.

(Hebrews 10:17 KJV)

In whom ye also trusted, after that ye heard the word of truth, the gospel of your salvation: in whom also after that ye believed, ye were sealed with that holy Spirit of promise,

(Ephesians 1:13 KJV)

And be not conformed to this world: but be ye transformed by the renewing of your mind, that ye may prove what is that good, and acceptable, and perfect, will of God.

(Romans 12:2 KJV)

I am the true vine, and my Father is the
husbandman.

(John 15:1 KJV)

Chapter 10: Remember the Benefits

For God so loved the world, that he gave
his only begotten Son, that whosoever believeth in him should not perish, but have
everlasting life.

(John 3:16 KJV)

For he hath made him to be sin for us, who
knew no sin; that we might be made the
righteousness of God in him.

(2 Corinthians 5:21 KJV)

And so it is written, The first man Adam
was made a living soul; the last Adam was
made a quickening spirit.

(1 Corinthians 15:45 KJV)

Christ hath redeemed us from the curse of
the law, being made a curse for us: for it is
written, Cursed is every one that hangeth
on a tree: That the blessing of Abraham
might come on the Gentiles through Jesus

Christ; that we might receive the promise
of the Spirit through faith. And if ye be
Christ's, then are ye Abraham's seed, and
heirs according to the promise.

(Galatians 3:13–14, 29 KJV)

And almost all things are by the law
purged with blood; and without shedding
of blood is no remission.

(Hebrews 9:22 KJV)

Let us labour therefore to enter into that
rest, lest any man fall after the same example of unbelief.

(Hebrews 4:11 KJV)

Don't worry about anything; instead, pray
about everything. Tell God what you need,
and thank him for all he has done.

(Philippians 4:6 NLT)

Preserve me, O God: for in thee do I put
my trust.

(Psalm 16:1 KJV)

REFERENCES

"Bethel Music: Goodness of God by Brian Johnson, Jason Ingram, Ed Cash, Ben Fielding, and Jenn Johnson." 2019. Azlyrics.com. 2019. https://www.azlyrics.com/lyrics/bethelmusic/goodnessofgod.html.

Chapman, Gary. 2005. *The Four Seasons of Marriage: Secrets to a Lasting Marriage*. Carol Stream: Tyndale House Publishers. https://store.iblp.org/the-four-seasons-of-marriage-softcover.html.

Copeland, Kenneth, and Gloria Copeland. 2012. *Limitless Love: A 365-Day Devotional*. Updated edition. Harrison House Publishers.

Diblasio, Frederick. 2000. "Decision-Based Forgiveness Treatment in Cases of Marital Infidelity." *Psychotherapy: Theory, Research, Practice, Training* 37 (2): 150. https://doi.org/10.1037/h0087834.

Evans, Jimmy. 1996. *Marriage on the Rock: God's Design for Your Dream Marriage*. Majestic Media.

Webster, Noah. 2022a. "Conditional." In *Noah Webster American Dictionary of the English Language: Webster's Online Dictionary 1828*, Online Edition. https://websters-dictionary1828.com/Dictionary/Conditional.

———. 2022b. "Unconditional." In *Noah Webster American Dictionary of the English Language: Webster's Online Dictionary 1828*, Online. https://webstersdictionary1828.com/Dictionary/unconditional.

Winston, Bill. 2019. *Vengeance of the Lord*. Oak Park: Bill Winston Ministries.

ABOUT THE AUTHOR

LeVonda G. Brown, a native of Washington, D.C., is pursuing her marriage and family therapist license. LeVonda received her bachelor's degree from Hope College and her master's in Marriage and Family Therapy from Liberty University. LeVonda retired from the Federal government, where she served as a Senior Analyst/Enforcement Officer and a collateral Equal Employment Opportunity (EEO) counselor and mediator.

LeVonda and her husband are anointed by God to serve as relationship counselors, including marriage, pre-marital, family, parent-child, friendships, and the workplace. For nearly seven years, they served as leaders of the Marriage Ministry at their local church. They enjoy sharing biblical principles with couples, families, and individuals in explaining the best way to work toward a healthy and mature relationship with the Lord.

LeVonda is married to Kenneth. They have two married children, Timothy (Kimberly) and Krystal (Brian), and two granddaughters.

Printed in the USA
CPSIA information can be obtained
at www.ICGtesting.com
CBHW052054241024
16329CB00023B/475